Jennifer

by

SHAN PECK

ISBN-13: 978-1519205537

DEDICATION

This book is for Jennifer, my strongest artistic
inspiration in the 1990's, while living in coastal Santa Barbara, California.

ACKNOWLEDGMENTS

I would like to acknowledge Adult education team in Santa Barbara, California. I have been participating in classes at the Schott and Wake center for many years. I have met lot of great artists, models, and lectors. Thank you!

Morlie

Shan Peck

Design

Autumn 2015 Art

Fine Art Auction

By

Shan Peck

Featured Artists

JUKKA NOPSANEN - FINLAND

RERA KRYZHNAYA - RUSSIA

JANET LAVIDA - U.S.A.

JILIAN CRAMB - U.S.A.

PAMELA MEREDITH - AUSTRALIA

MICK WILIAMS - U.S.A.

DENISE FULMER - U.S.A.

PAMELA CLEMENTS - U.S.A.

LIDIA ESSEN - RUSSIA

GARY SLUZEWSKI - U.S.A.

TIMOTHY HACKER - U.S.A.

MARGARET BROOKS - SAINT MARTIN

PAT GEHR - U.S.A.

DONNA COOK - U.S.A.

ROBERT YAEGER - U.S.A.

LOIS VIGUIER - FRANCE

JAYNE SOMOGY - U.S.A.

Dushan

Design

Winter 2015 Art

Fine Art Auction

by

Shan Peck

ISBN 9781522930129

9 781522 930129

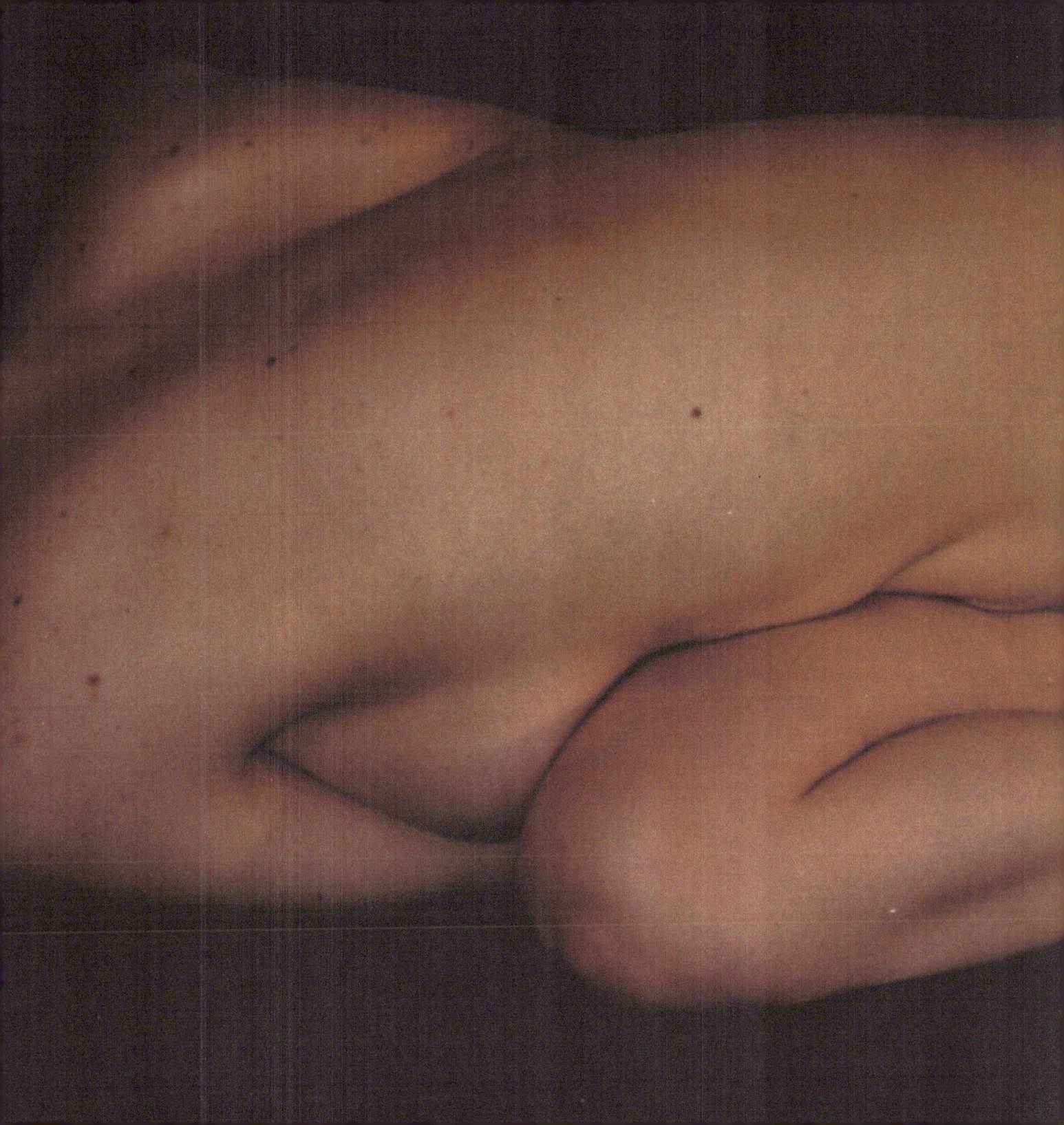

JENNIFER

It was already six months that I was visiting sculpture class at the Adult Education program. Old high school was used for few dozens of classes. After when I experienced drawing, painting, theatre, piano and computer class, I wanted to challenge myself with a sculpture class. It was not even my idea. It was my Dutch friend Maria that suggested this art class. I wanted her to join me for a drawing and painting classes, which I was taking already for several years, but she insisted that we take a sculpture class.

In this class we got a clay that you could later procure in the oven and your art work after some surface painting or patina application, it ended up as good as something that you would buy in the store. That is, if you were good enough. I was never good enough. My hands were not able to blend the mass of clay into something that would look as model at front of us.

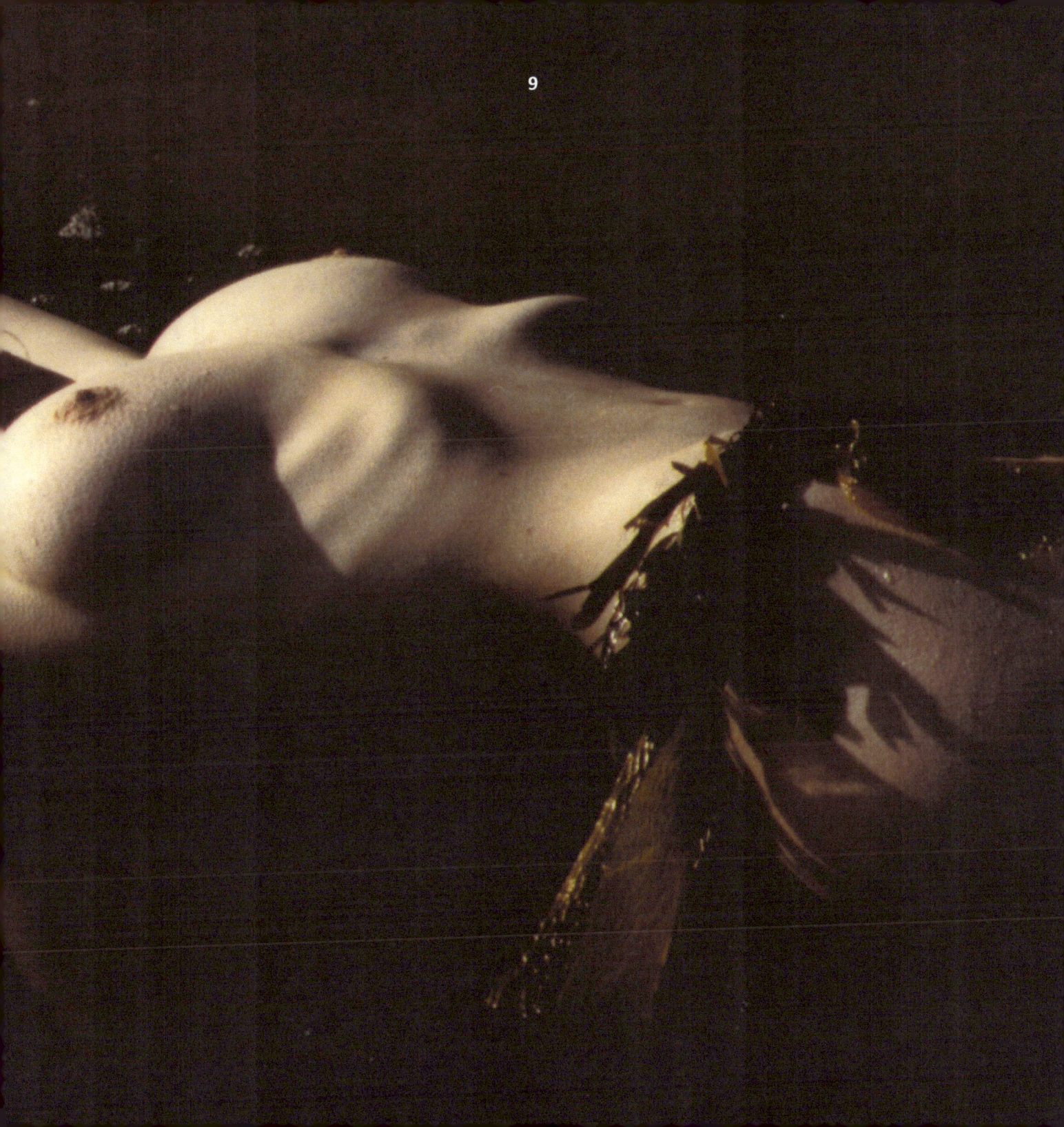

JENNIFER

We sculpted by observing nude female or male model, standing, seating or laying at front of us. The instructor for this class was a woman; she liked to come to student of her choice, so she could praise the art work and give some advice. Instructor did this only for a people that already did good job, which was kind of weird for me. I would come as instructor, to somebody that needs a help and is doing bad job. Well… Go figure.

Every time when the instructor went to someone, I got little jealous and the following week, I wanted to come with something that would be good enough for her to come to me and make some comments. Six months and nothing had happened at my work table. Maria got already her comments, I was there, just to have fun and the chance that I do make some wonderful work of art, I guess this chance was as small as the room we were in.

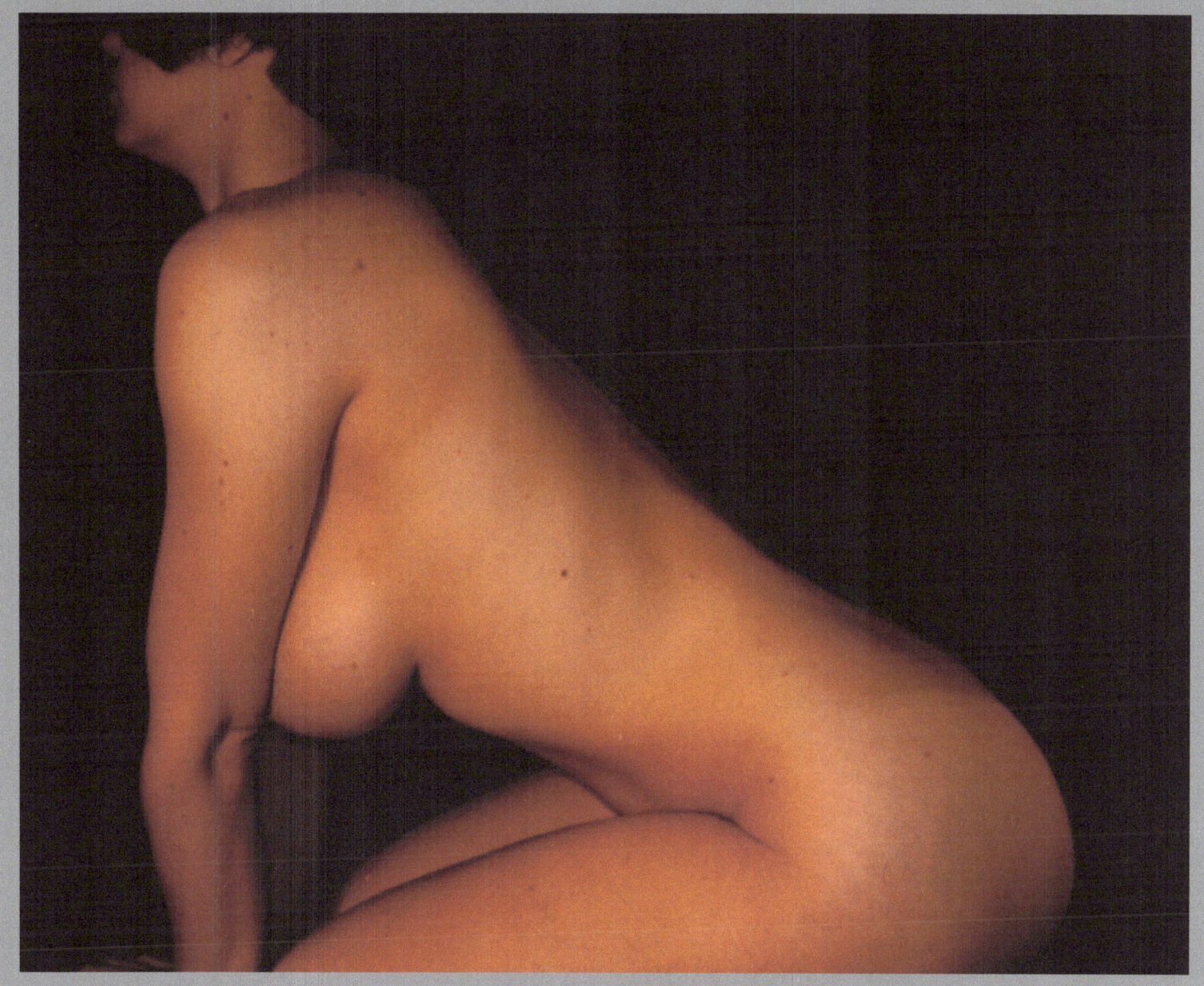

JENNIFER

The space where we created art works from live model, it was around eight by five yards. Attached to this room, it was another smaller room, where the finished sculptures were located or rather stored for a next week continuation. Also running water was in the smaller room, so you did not have to go to your car with dirty hands from greasy clay.

Outside of the sculpture room, it was smoking area and also a bench, little to the left toilettes and of course quiet big parking lot for few hundred cars. The group in which I was participating, it was every week different. People usually came in large numbers at the registration point and later when they got already in, they did chose to be in the class, based on time availability or maybe even based on the type of the model that we got during the twelve weeks period that this sculpture class lasted.

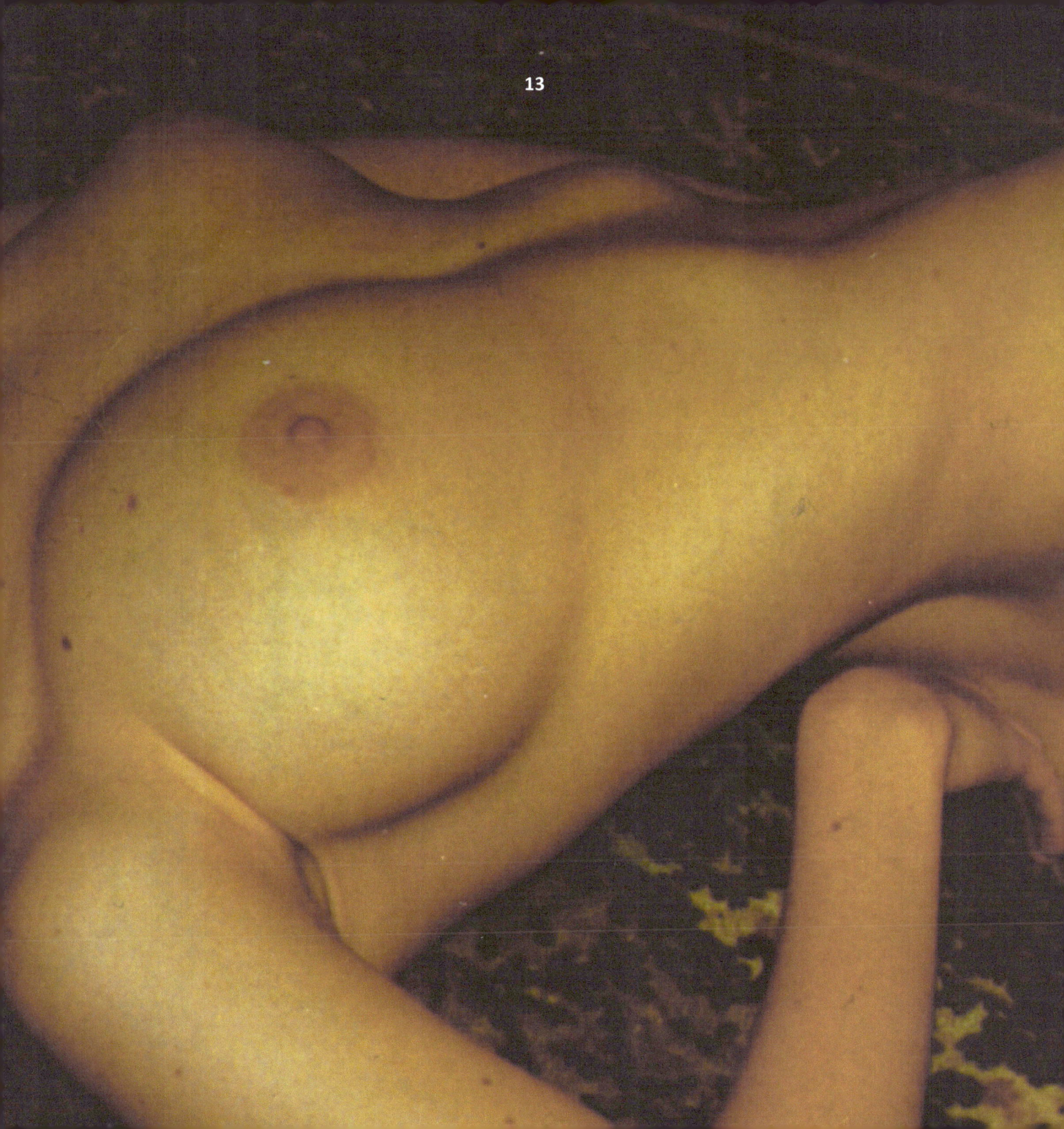

JENNIFER

To my largest artistic orgasm to the date, the instructor came to me in my second set of twelve week sculpture class. She said few very encouraging words and asked me few questions and after few minutes, she was on her way to talk to somebody else. This was my fifteen minutes of being somebody or famous as Andy Warhol said once, everybody will be famous for fifteen minutes. I had no clue why she came to me at that day, why not some other day or other course, or other model…I found this out after few years. It was tall and voluptuous young woman, age below twenty. I think still upper teen years she had and later I found out that she was a student at the college, paying for her school by modeling in drawing and painting classes and also this sculpture class. Her name was Jennifer. She had beautiful long hair, dark and straight. Wide hips and thin waist. Pear like beautiful breast that slightly were falling down but not from being older, but because of their size simply, they could not possibly stay straight, with nipples pointing directly at front.

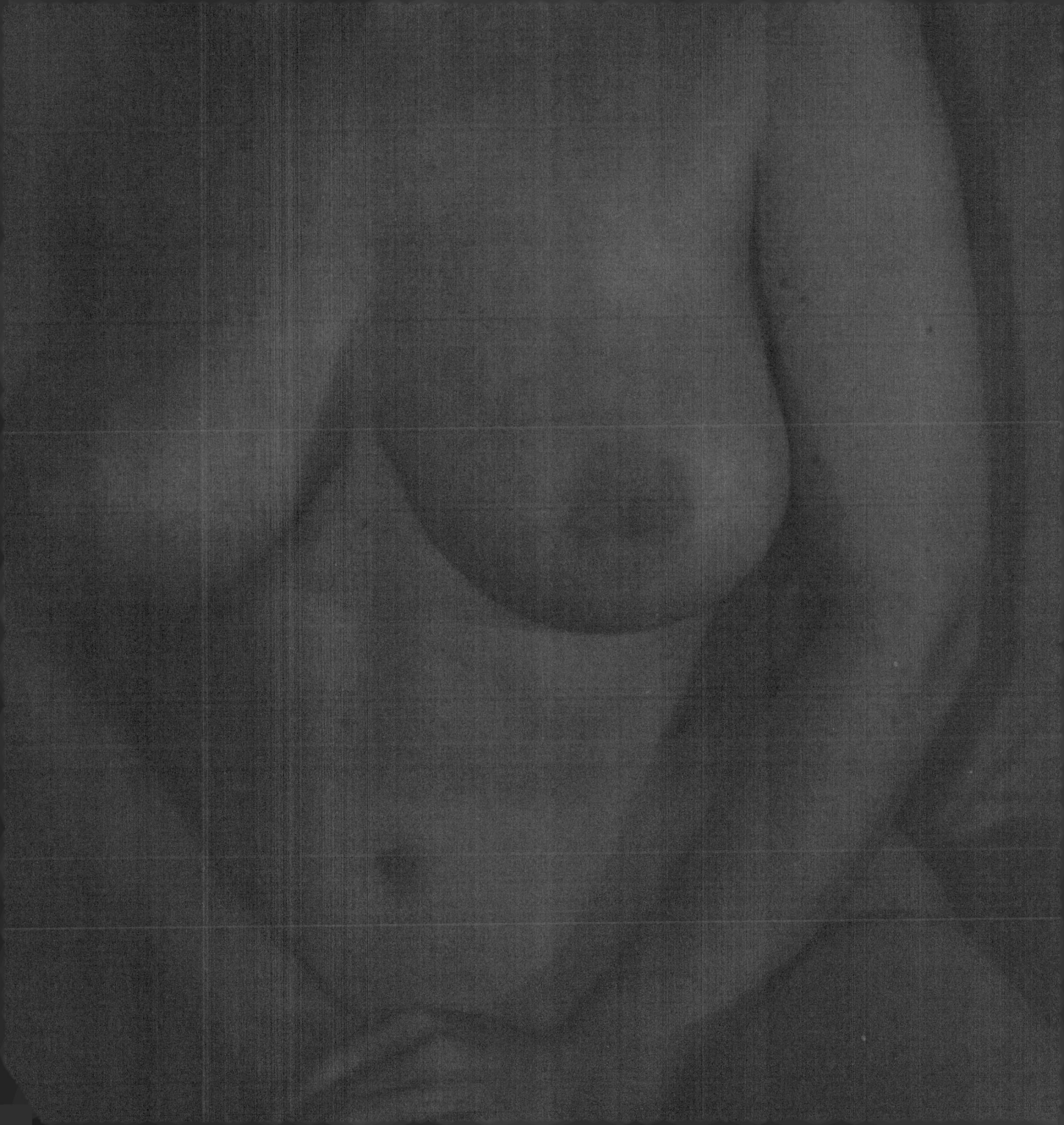

JENNIFER

The bottom of the breast was going up again, what I am calling, the returning pear shaped breast. Jennifer was very pale as far her skin of her body. She told me later that she disliked spending longer time in the sun, so she doesn't look like those typical California women in their sixties when skin is covered with red dots that represent strong possibility for melanoma illness and as far the female beauty, doesn't look good at all.

At the end of that sculpture class where I captured attention of my female instructor, I asked if the model that we just got, will come again next week. I was told that she will come and be with us for few more times in the near future. Our work or rather experimentation with clay, it took more than just one three hour session, time range that average class was lasting. So I was glad that Jennifer will be present and with us, even next week.

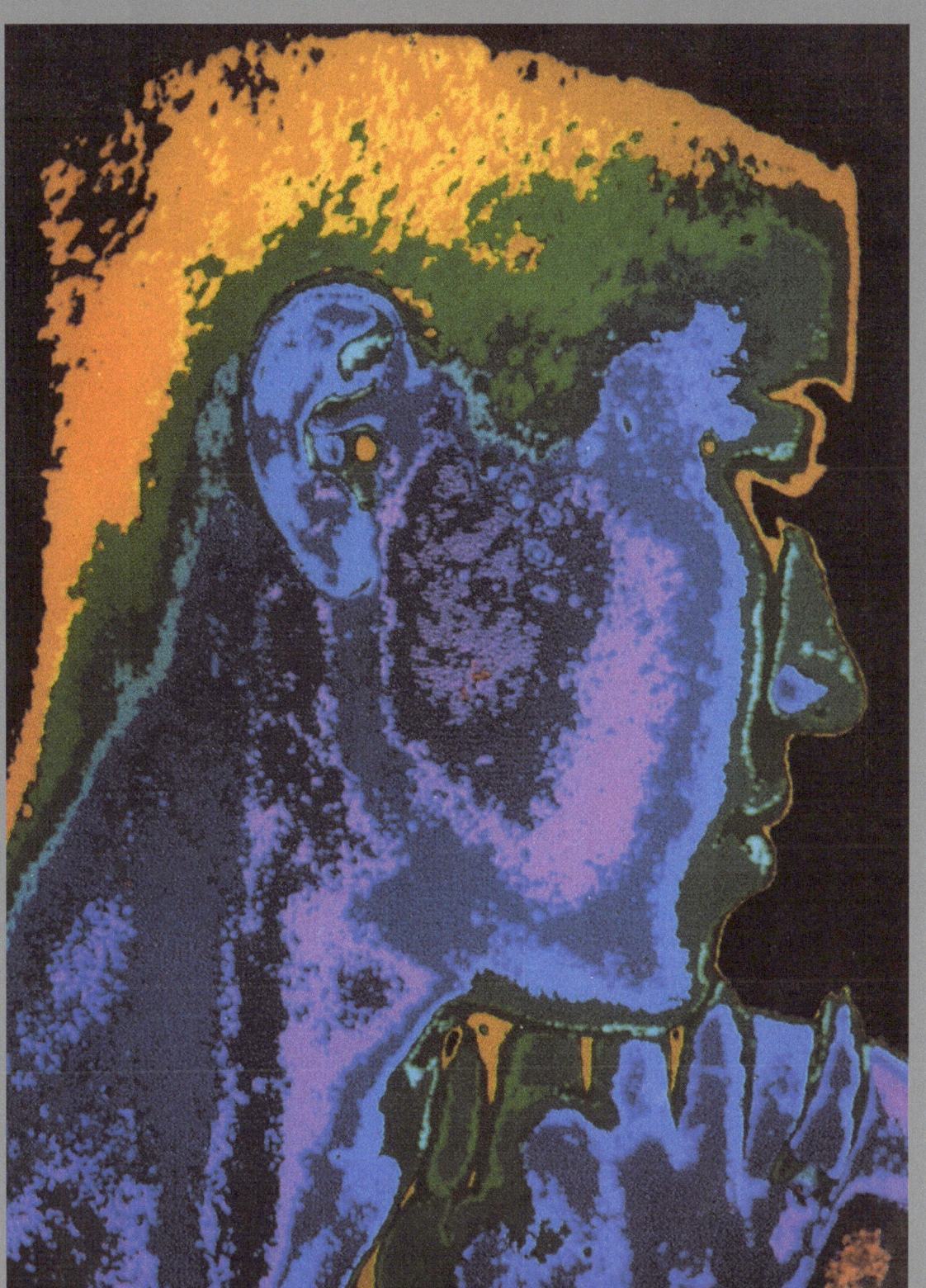

JENNIFER

I used to take my finished sculpture to my home and worked on it just from a memory. In this case, I left it in the class and with excitement, waited for Jennifer to appear again. She was one of the best looking models as far the type of the figure goes. She was a proud owner of the hourglass body shape. But she was not using this figure for her advantage, she dressed in baggy clothing and she did all this to cover her beauty with intention to have peace and quiet in her life. Men are horrible in this aspect. When a man sees woman who is gorgeous and he would like to get her into the bed, he usually bugs her to the point that he destroys any chance for him and her to be friends. My strategy was completely different. If I wanted a woman to end up with me at the horizontal tango, I accepted that after one big, but very clear and honest trial, I will back up and leave her alone, if rejected. This was my major at the Landmark Education experience. Be OK with rejection and accept answer NO as it would be yes.

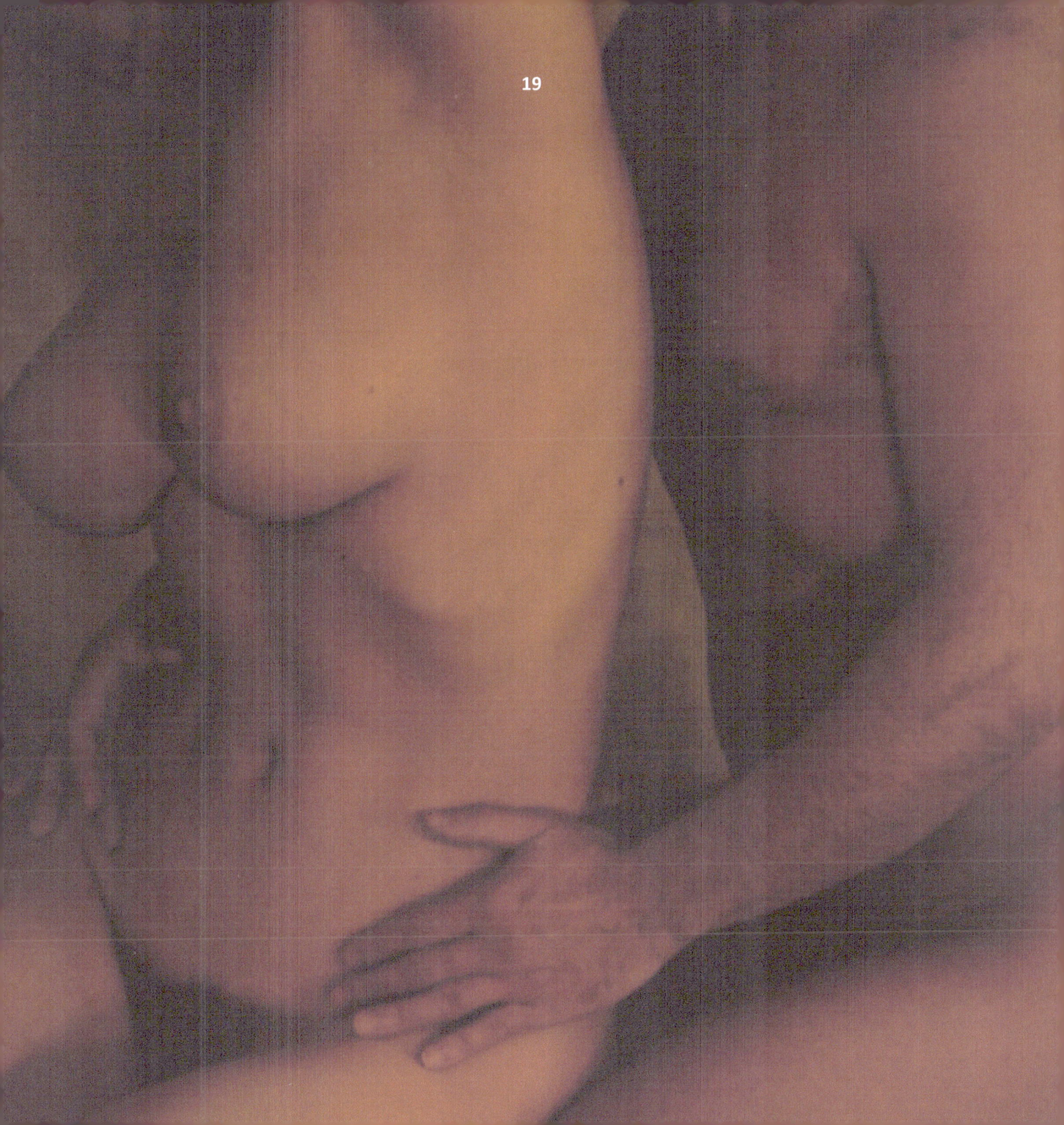

JENNIFER

I separated women by interest or rather type of activities that I wanted to have with them. Jennifer was in category of artistic projects. I am sure that even if she wanted to have an intimate relationship with me, that I would rather be an idiot and maybe even played a role of a gay, just to prevent myself from losing this huge energy field that attracted me to Jennifer. Also I was thankful for having chance to work with her for so long time, because it kept me from bars and drinking and kept me behind my canvases and also at front of the camera.

From the time when I met Jennifer first time, few weeks passed and I prepared myself to show her some of my art works, also wanted to request from her, if she would consider to pose nude for me for fine art photography sessions and also for live painting, all in my studio at my home. Those few works that I was able to show her, it was from photography sessions with Mary Ann.

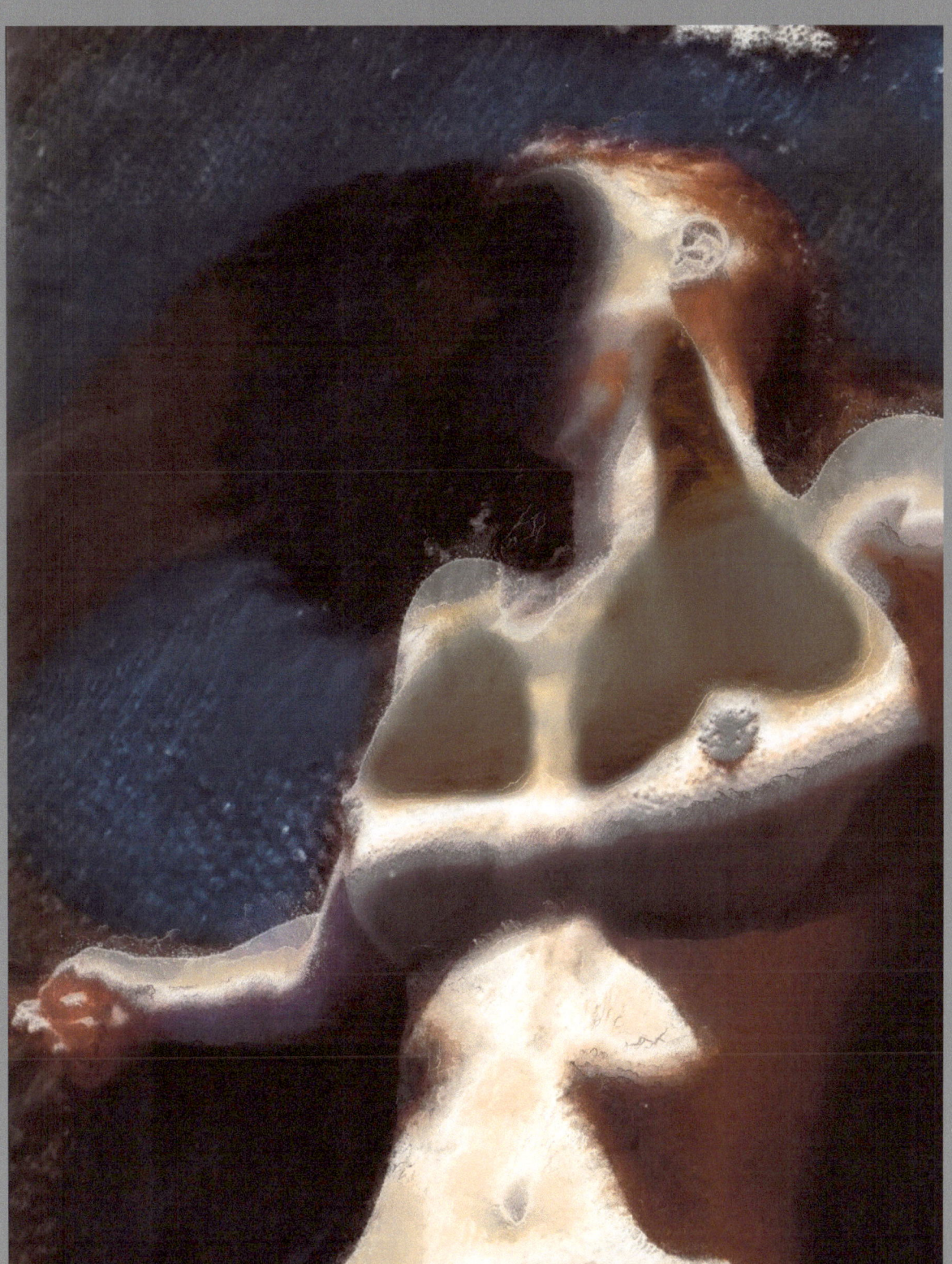

JENNIFER

Some of the photos ended to have some computer manipulation done, but there were no hand drawings or paintings that I could show at that time. Jennifer said OK, to my surprise. I was very excited to have her available in the near future, wanted to do my best while working with her. When I went home, I started to think, what I could possibly do for a background, during photography sessions. I bought large dark green bed cloth. Also I had this woven blanket in king size and not last; I was preparing to use also white bed sheets.

My first session with Jennifer was little shy and careful. I had no idea what I can allow my self to ask her, what poses we can get into. Jennifer was poser that did not need much guidance. Most of the poses that we did, she created herself and there was no need to request any adjustments or to push her to do more than we did already.

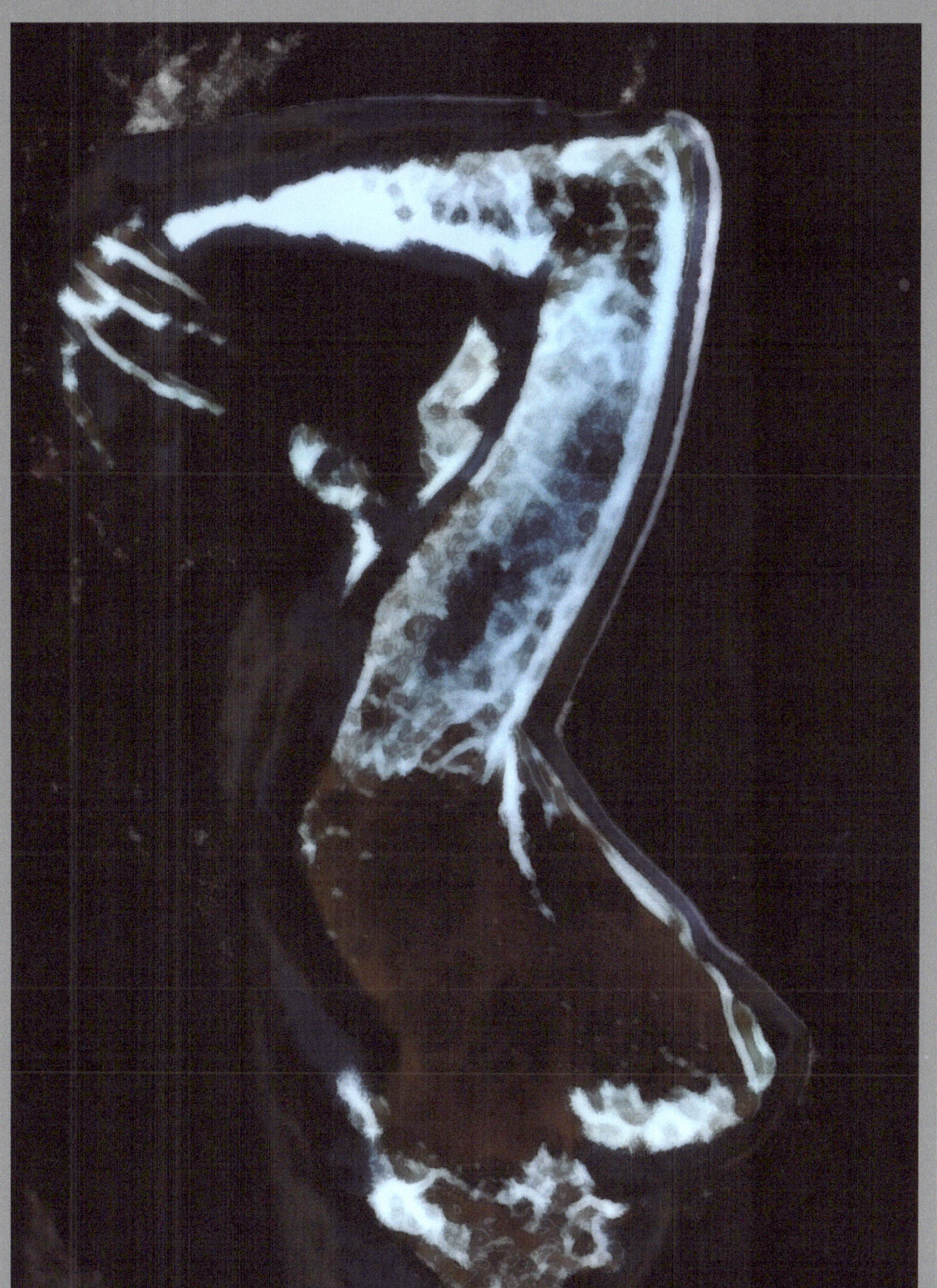

JENNIFER

Jennifer besides the modeling job, she worked at the Borders bookstore. She had her responsibilities in there as most of the employees, place the books on the shelves and keep the space clean and in order. Beside this, she also had an art consultant function. When I managed to have enough of nerve to go to the Borders bookstore to ask if they would consider me for one month of art showing on their walls, it was also after Jennifer encouraged me to do so. She told me who is the person in charge and what should I bring as samples. I meet this man and showed him my portfolio of art works. To my huge surprise, he asked me "Would you like June or July? " I picked up the earliest possible date, so I answer that I want a June. It was sometimes in April and I had some six weeks, before I was supposed to hang my art works in this huge, three floors bookstore where only twelve people during the year, had the privilege to show their art.

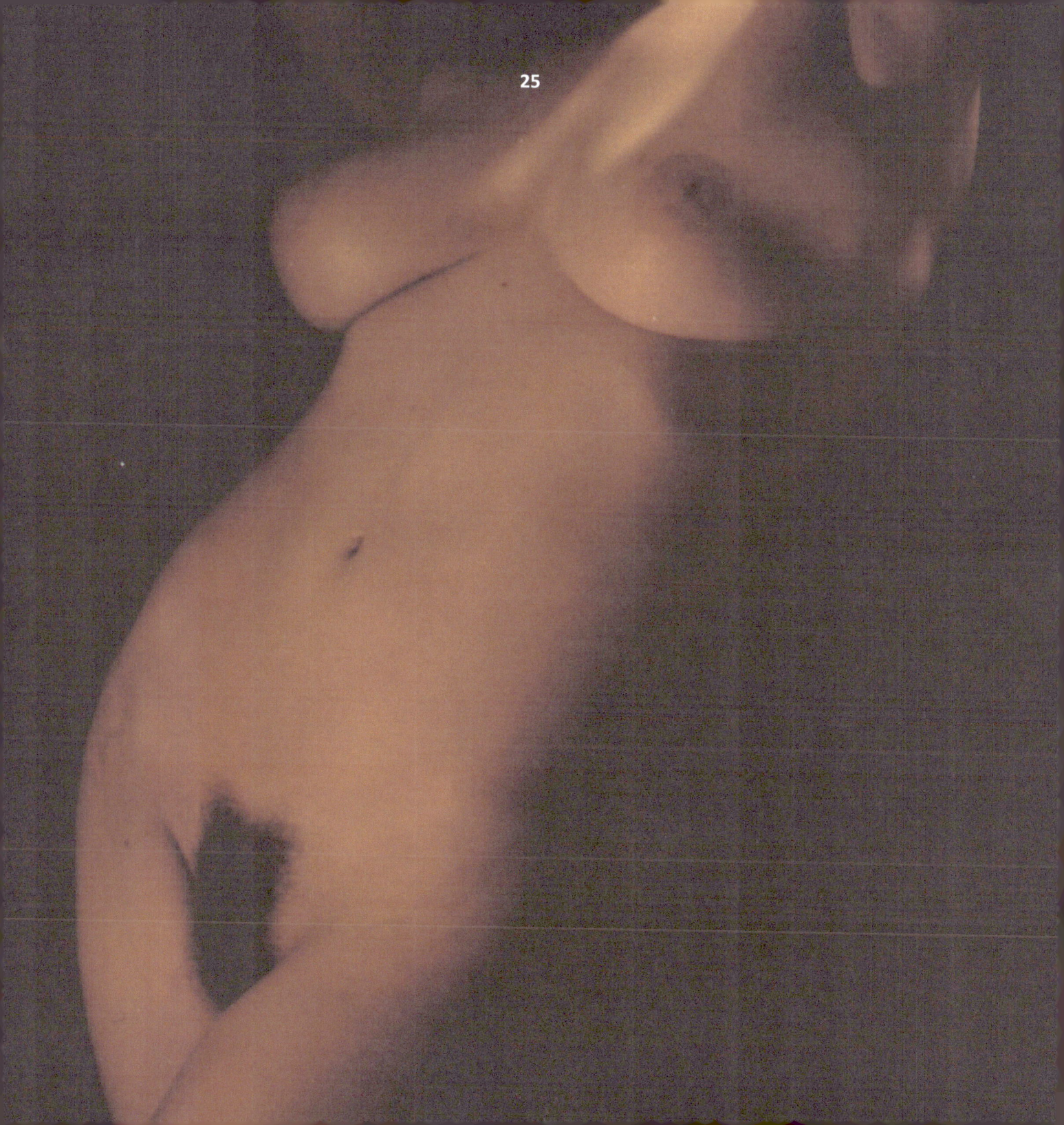

JENNIFER

To sell my work, that was one of my strongest motivations, since I was in my mind still poor and at the edge of society, expensive living in Santa Barbara, always close to be a homeless person. Only the fact that America was in the 90's, in two wars in Iraq, only that kept me employed and with some money in my pocket. Santa Barbara is very cruel town to poor people. Imagine to live in place which everyone calls a paradise, when you don't have enough money to pay fourteen hundred dollars rent for two bedroom apartment and have to be inside of the paradise to look around how the top ten percent is having good time in open air street restaurants, theatre and other places offering good quality entertainment for top dollars that you do not have.

Jennifer was the only reason why I stayed in this town during period of three years. Last I did hear about her, she moved to San Francisco to study architecture. Maybe one day she will be in a bookstore and she will notice this book on the shelf...

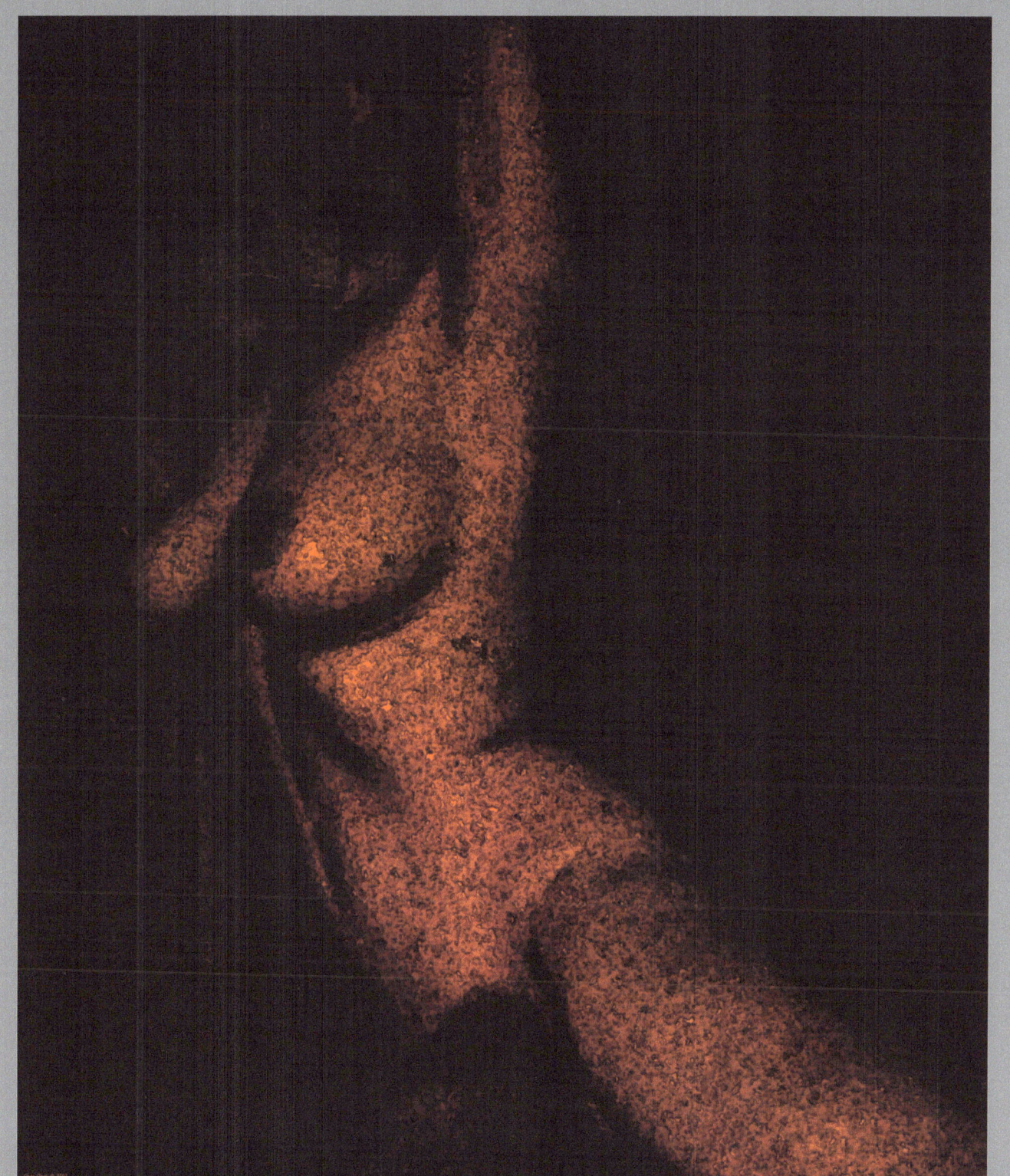

ABOUT THE AUTHOR

At the age of 15, he started to write short stories, poems, screen plays. When 19 of age, worked as technician at the film studios, department for special effects and light. Worked also on movie Amadeus, directed by Oscar winning director, Milos Forman. At age 24, emigrated to United States. In 1989 moved to California where he joined theatre group Gilbert & Sullivan. During his stay in California went to Santa Barbara Community College where he visited several accredited courses as Business law and Design. After death of his father in 2001, he returned to his birth country where he worked as Quality Engineer, Quality Assurance manager and Manufacturing Project Manager. In quality assurance he got Black Belt / 6 Sigma training while working in automotive industry.

He had few art shows in Europe and United States. On top of fine art painting, he also started to do sculptures and the other strong activity that he spent a lot of time with – design inventions, technical and design improvements in fields like optics, acoustics and motion picture E^2E^2 systems. Currently he writes his second book which is also written in parallel, as screen play for the film.

E MAIL CONTACT: motyl_1999@yahoo.com

www.ingramcontent.com/pod-product-compliance
Lightning Source LLC
Chambersburg PA
CBHW050424180526
45159CB00005B/2395